Pick Apart My Brain and You Will Find

Madeleine Misner

Presentation by *BookLeaf Publishing*

Web: www.bookleafpub.com

E-mail: info@bookleafpub.com

ISBN: 9789363309050

First edition 2024

to Hazel

ACKNOWLEDGEMENT

thank you to the English Department at Loyola Marymount University, all my friends for dealing with all my "Maddy Stories", my parents for never settling on one place, and Isabel Eccles, for the author picture.

PREFACE

These poems are dramatic, sad, and hopefully make you chuckle at their relatability, at times. Other times, they are windows into the writer's personal life and her reflections. She hopes you take the bluntness with hints of sarcasm, but also retrospective clarity. Pick Apart My Brain and You Will Find is meant for the reader with an acute sense of hyper-awareness of the laughable dramedy that deals with unearthing big emotions. Please enjoy and feel free to laugh, with a grain of salt.

Chicken Caesar Salad

See, God!
I'm eating a chicken Caesar salad!

I made the chicken myself:
First, I preheated the oven to 450 degrees, and
while I waited for that to come up to
temperature,
Washed the cutlets off, pounded them flat,
breaded them, and placed them on the rack,
All by myself!

They cooked for 30 minutes, and no fatty oil
was needed,
I made the salad using a Trader Joe's salad kit,
and didn't even include the croutons!
Those useless, hard-cubed carb bombs.

I chilled the salad in a big bowl in the fridge,
and then cut up the chicken,
And I actually remembered to let the meat rest
for five minutes after cooking,
Then ate half a chicken breast and half the salad
kit and
Saved the rest for later!

Aren't you so proud, capital D Daddy-o,
That I've made this nutritious and delicious
baked chicken Caesar salad,
And washed my hands before and after dinner
and thanked you for
Chickens and Trader Joes.

Can you send me some good luck now?

AAAAAAAAAmen.

I don't get embarrassed

much,
anymore. I have decided to
forfeit that feeling. Decided,
oh that? That's useless. After all,
isn't my body and mind just here for
a limited time only? And that judgment or
eating a cupcake or writing a shitty poem
will evaporate into the stars in
sixty years time,
if I'm lucky.

(I don't even like cupcakes, it's just to prove a
point)

No, but yes. That statement of 'living on a
floating rock' is pretty useful, whereas, like
previously stated, embarrassment is not.

However,

I have decided to forfeit the actions,
those useless but tried-and-true patterns,
that have led me to embarrassment before.
Rather, lean on yourself,
lean into yourself,

the dark patches of the self, they hide behind
your liver and lungs,

(because embarrassment is just the default after
moments lacking confidence, moments where
you wonder what decision you would have made
if you just honed in on how the soles of your feet
felt pressed in your shoes, standing on the
ground)

and replace them with daisy chains and cooking
salmon,
speaking your mind even if you have to cry it
out later;

I've heard it's better to speak than to die,
Haven't we all?
The 'I love you's trapped in my breath remind
me of that,
The stories written on a post-it note that I threw
away with last week's trash remind me of that,
Writing shitty poetry reminds me –
The leaves will change whether I'm cowering in
bed or raking them up.

The Ants Come Marching
One by One

I am made of the ants in my room,
Staring at the ambivalent (sometimes) giant
Looming over their   faces   ?

They crawl in and out of my ears, my nostrils,
As I sleep, oversleep, undereat,
And stall.
Forgetting to feed them their sweet traps,
So therefore they take over.

One, by one, in the corners of the room,
The sugar ants,
Shiny black and constant,
Have not given me one break.

This one is surveying my work, judging my
sexual encounters,
And has triumphed all over my windowpane and
bookshelf.

I feel nothing but phantom legs, crawling,
dragging, all over my brain.
Slap my neck and pull back a hand of bent
bodies,

Bouncing back to life, they take a beating or two
to die.

The military lines are better for me, one spurting
spray,
Off-brand Raid does the job, nicely, for a
moment.
There's organization in this part of the battle.
Sporadic ones, they irk me.
Broken away from their colony (it's in the
floor!),
They exist to kill me – slowly, one by one,
through
Mental warfare.

I get rid of them only for two or five or seven
strays to wink,
The shimmy of tiny legs crawling over my
comforter,
Beating me in game they aren't aware of.

They exist, they have a goal – food.
They are doing better than me.

Trade In

Throw away the rusted bell,
Picked from the treasure box in Mrs. B's fourth
grade class,
Only because it sounded like it had a soul,
Somewhere in the tarnished silver.

I have to declutter to feel free.
I'm used to hanging on,
Gripping to A+ papers, restaurant drawings,
Ticket stubs, gum wrappers, receipts with
lipstick stains.
A trash bag is my newest weapon,
There's strength in releasing a grip,
Letting the contents fall into black polyethylene
plastic.

To declutter is to clear:
Trinkets usually adorn my shelves,
Fill boxes in the corners of my closet,
I was never good at sitting in silence,
But also,
Yes,
I was,
I'm quiet when I'm decorating. My mind is quiet
when I'm getting rid of solitude.

When I'm smoking weed or having sex or
running,
It's quiet.
It started with decorating,
Which started with collecting,
Which started with assigning importance to
moments that should not be more than a
memory.

I'm trading them in.
I'm decluttering the old,
I'm ringing in the new, I'm bringing in solitude,
I'm only allowing self-sufficiency.
I'm running from the memories, from the
popcorn lung,
From the pain in my side that persists after every
time they leave – and they will leave.

I'm trading it all in.

Things I Have Said:

(over the phone to my best friend) I woke up this
morning to my cat shitting on the stairs.

(in a Starbucks before school in the 10th grade) I
only drink black coffee.

(in the title of a previously written poem) I have
a problem with intimacy.

(on a weekend trip with my ex-boyfriend…)
Give me a hug and I'll turn my head away.

(…and after he asked if that was a song lyric)
No, but I am going to write that down.

(over text before a long night) Don't worry, I
will not let myself be a rebound.

(laying staring at the ceiling of a Venice
apartment) Can we go on an actual date now?

(on the dancefloor of a Santa Monica bar) You
look like you're about to kiss me.

(under my covers in the morning) Your eyes are
very pretty.

(while sobbing outside the Church on campus)
Just give me one thing!

(over the text conversation that inspired this
poem) I love vulnerability, I just don't like being
held accountable.

I have a memory of the boy I did not like:

His eyebrows were furrowed, pulled together
downwards,
So concentrated, not angry, but looking it.
His mouth was a tight line, lips parted slightly,
For air to escape.
I looked at the muscles bordering his mouth and
chin,
The parallel lines, what are those called?
The ones that make a mouth manly.

I remember stopping – stopping trying,
I did not care about pleasure all of a sudden.
His eyes were not on my face, as I said,
He was concentrating,
I felt the wrinkles in my face relax, in curiosity.
I let myself just look up.

I had one thought: he looks beautiful.
It was simple, true.
Sometimes I wish he knew that.
Sometimes I wonder if it was me who couldn't
make it work,
Deciding it was me,
And wonder,

Just wonder,
I wonder,

honestly

I do not know.

Layers

This building upon this self –
Loam and clay in the dirt,
Different colored and textured,
Staining the palms red, the thickness of clay,
Sticking to itself layer after layer,
Fossils deep under bedrock under clay under
loam under soil,
I do not know the truth of it,
Or where it starts, perhaps it just falls out the
other end,
Upside down with the penguins in the arctic,
Turning cold and icy, the blues of an unearthed
iceberg
Topsy-turvy, toppled over itself,
I am not sure which tragedy I am crying for or
angry for anymore.

The bite mark on your arm,
I only saw it in the morning,
And went silent, radio, static in my ears,
The rush of the blood in my ears,
Debating how, not if, to ask what it is,
Wondering are you crazy enough to bite your
own arm,
And I know my mouth was nowhere near there.

The flower in the corner of the windshield with a
smiley face,
I was never good at drawing, I have my own
style,
This was not mine, my flowers are eerie,
God it's making me hot even now,
Hot like the heat on blast in the car
Revealing pink color in my cheeks,
I just silently pointed at it,
You said it was your sister who did it,
But why would she be in the passenger seat?
You hated sharing the car with her,
We fucked in her bed.

Why would you try to hold two, or more, things
at once?
I never understood that.

I saw all of these things, silent, knowing,
knowing I am too smart to find another
loophole,
I was the one who offered them to you, you
couldn't even come up with excuses on your
own.
It makes me hot even now.
Silent, knowing, knowing what I was doing was
just hurting myself hurting myself hurting
myself because I needed something something

something else something to come easy, but easy
does not mean fruitful.

Easy does not mean fruitful.

Easy meant looking the other way,
Rubbing clay between your fingers until it
crumbled away,
There were no good days.
There were no good days.
I stayed.
Easy.

I stayed easy.
I don't understand holding two things at once.

Ocean Beach in Late 2020

One of my favorite memories
Involves spontaneous fireworks,
A dark, windy beach,
And one of the only times
I caught you looking at me first.

We were there – you, me, Abby,
Having driven all the way out –
The waves only appearing as oncoming
whitecaps, crashing noisily,
Almost louder than our silly conversation,
Whatever it was that made us laugh in the
moment,
Before a boom lit up the sky,
Our shoulders turning backwards first, us all
Flinging our gazes to the direction of the sound
–

    A big, red peony opening up the clouds.

It was so dark on the beach,
Barely able to see the whites of our eyes as we
huddled,
The firework revealed our pale chins pulled up,
And I turned to look back at you,
To look at you looking at the fireworks –

But your eyes were only on me:
Me – in the glow of the firework on the dark
windy beach, smiling and turning in slow
motion to look in stupid awe at our cosmic
timing here on the beach and the firework going
off and it was not a holiday or summertime, it
was fall in fact, and we came here on a whim
because we were all tired of being cooped up
and we had big jackets on and my hair was
being flung in all sorts of directions and I turned
to look at you as if to say, wow, look at that! but
your head was level, not looking up even
remotely,

And you were looking at me.

I am not pretty

I am not soft.

I am not whimsical.

I do not have the vocabulary or focus to hone in
on the veins in the petals of a marigold and
compare the pollen spores to life itself.

I use words like fuck and shit, and my poems
would scare my grandma.

My soul does not huff and sigh.

I think being blunt is an artform in itself.

If I am not bleeding, I am not being true,
And I think you're weird for hiding behind a
color pallet.

I hope to learn to conceal myself in my writing
later, down the line, when I have cashmere
cardigans hanging in my closet, with crows feat
deepening by my eyes.

Today is not that day,

I am not pretty,
I am not soft.

Heatwave

The air is soup,
Hot, thick, soup like soup can be when you're
sick
With the flu, and it's the only thing you can keep
down, and you've developed
A taste for only sodium and broth, and it needs
to be absolutely scalding and steaming.

Each breath feels like opening up, taking it in,
Parting damp thighs, peeling them off of the
cream leather seats of your teenage car,
Licking lips over and over again because, well,
You're parched.

The cars even move lazily,
Hanging like flies still in the air over cow shit,
the grass doesn't move today,
Limbs lay like a renaissance painting, and the
spiders,
All of them,
Crawl out of their hiding places into the shade,
Even they are sweating.

You touch yourself and become hot because
everything else is,

Biting down on the cracking lip, curling toes and
remembering every hand on
Every part of your body that's ever been grazed.
A vanilla Coca-Cola will not cure this type of
heat,
The sweetness helps to quell, something to
dance on the tongue.

God, I'm so hot,
I just gasp,
Clutch,
Drag the nails across,
Claw,
Scratch
at my own
skin.

Blackout

Listening to the breeze build up, flow above my head, only signified by the rubbing together of leaves – distant first, but then crescendoing into visibility, the silhouette of the branches move.

It's ungodly quiet, what I would imagine the ninth day was like, creation just stirring, waiting in the first moments of breath.

The only light is a peach ember, burning like how a symphony hums, at the end of my cigarette. Then a second, a third.

It's hot, a summer evening that makes you feel wrong to be alone. It is wrong to be alone, but my call will not go through. The power took down the streetlights and stop signs; there's no way to contact you.

I imagine you sitting in the chair opposite from me, somehow I can see your eyes. I'm waiting for you to come kiss me, sober, under the stars.

A pipe dream. One in which I have to listen to my heartbeat and hug my left arm to come back

to my body, remind myself it's not healthy to
daydream these things. Somehow the dark
makes me think you can feel these thoughts, too.
I wish you to be in agony over it, too.

A candle flickers on the counter inside. It's for
my cats, so they know the dark is not my doing.
I only burned it for them.

To be unloved has never felt so alive, and I'm
waiting for you in the dark. I'm waiting for you
to look at the stars and think of me, too. I'm
waiting in the blackout for you to show up at my
door. I'm waiting, because now I know that I
can. I'm waiting, I'm feeling the breeze, I'm
looking at the stars,

I'm thinking of only your eyes.

The only thing I reach for is my computer -

I want a hug, I want to be held.
Arms are things I grab at in the dark, half-asleep,
Half-drunk, acceptable here.

I am the fall guy,
Throw me off a cliff, that's the only thing I'm
good for,
Hitting the jutted parts, spraining my elbow
stuck in crevices,
Clawing my hands to seem fierce – I am not,
Alone, I have to exhale alone,

Do you exist only to force me to be okay with
being alone?
Alone is a word I mastered at ten.
I am a resentful poet. My face is one adored by
leeches.
I am resentfully strong.

The tears will come, I will not let them breech.
One can fall, I'm tired of a wet face.
Another. I did not say okay to this.

Let us make jokes, is all I am a one-liner,

Something to let out a laugh over beer.

I am a half-way house for the final destination,
Reach out my hand for you to steady your
balance,
Push me under in the process,
Regain your footing,
Because I can hug myself.

Exhale,
That's all I know how to do,
Exhale.

My Soul Has a Hangover

I need to clean the house and make that corn and
black bean salad I bought the ingredients for

I need to text the people that I've been avoiding
that I need space and don't know why, I just do.

I need to let go of the one person who I write
poems about; he does not even have a contact
photo for my number.

I need to nap. I need money. I need to write, and
send emails. I need to read my emails.

I need to drink water and get back on Accutane.

My soul has a hangover and I cannot even feel
shame anymore,
I've doused myself in shame and
embarrassment,
Taken a million scalding hot showers,
Used up collective months' worth of sleeping it
off
Exhaled a breath of vowing 'never again' too
many times –
I wouldn't say I'm numb to it.

I'm the farthest from my eyes I've seen in a
while,
The sockets are their own purple valleys,
I'm aware better takes time,
Time ends up being my enemy,
Time makes me think it's over,
That the self-work has cemented:
It did not.

When I was younger I used to put myself in
time-outs because my emotions felt too big, and
that somehow felt wrong. Wrong enough to sit
on the landing of the stairs facing the wall, for
thirty minutes at a time.

I feel that coming on again.

The Gravedigger

I wrapped cinnamon rolls in cellophane,
Hoping the peel would keep the icing sticky,
Warm.

I like to keep things as they are,
Sixty seconds collected is my mortal enemy,
They swarm together like wasps,
One sting is fine – the whole hive banded
together means death.

My knuckles have surpassed white: blood
coagulates in bruises on each ridge.
The fingers are stuck in a rigor mortis-curl,
I'm crying as I'm saying sorry for hanging on.

I was the youngest in the gentle and restorative
yoga class,
My legs shook when holding them above my
head,
How could a body be so old so fast,
I even just corrected my posture while typing –
A person's desk will tell you when they will die.
My bottle of Excedrin migraine to the left,
A half-drunk coldening coffee sits in front of
me,

Between my chest and the computer screen.

Whenever I die,
I think my ghost will stay twenty-two.
She likes it here.

Mulberry Bush

I was toe-head blonde with a bob, once,
and pink corduroy shorts, an Old Navy shirt.
Grandma bought me a large Coca-Cola the size
of my head,
a king size tootsie roll,
a combination I haven't reproduced, but
remember so vividly,
fondly, nonetheless.

I would grab the chains of the tree swing so
tight,
so long, orange rust painted my palm sweat.
There's a broken down one-wood vineyard
in the back-backyard.
That part of the yard is where swing sets went to
die.
At the end of the driveway,
a mulberry bush.

My cousin and I had a profitable business,
for one day, and one day only, we made
'kid-wine',
sold it to our mouths.
We mixed the mushed buckets of collected
mulberries

with Raw sugar, emptying brown paper packets,
stirring and mulling the concoction.
The FDA shut us down, a green worm was
found
floating in the second batch.

My eyes are puffy today, my legs are two feet
longer.
I jumped into the community pool after the gym,
turns out 'not enough' is a mindset, not a
sweat-able toxin,
so I needed to float.
On the path back, dots of unripe red and
throbbing purples
appeared in the green like spots in my vision.
Mulberries.

Crouched, hair tangled and dripping, sunglasses
slipping off my face and pool bag slipping off
my shoulder, hunched, I pulled berry after berry
off the branches and suckled at the purple wine
bursting and settling into my fingerprints,
absorbing into my skin faster than my tongue
could grasp it. Mulberries, mulberries,
mulberries.

Bring me back to a summer where everything
was sweet.

Raincheck

I think
I saw one of those African-hornet
Dragon looking wasps
On my hike today.

The end is near,
But I just gave myself a blowout.
Can we post-pone Armageddon
For brunch next week?

Plums

Plums

I could handcraft artisan earrings, they fall apart
after four uses,
in the back of a van traversing over waterfalls
and fallen, lichen covered logs,
while writing my manuscript, ending up in San
Francisco, the city by the bay,
because I need to see water, and drift on over to
the beach towns down south –
      I've already done that one –
trying my hand at learning the bass, or maybe
drums would rather suit me,
perhaps I'd fully commit to purple hair, not
temporary wash-outable dye,
adding another tattoo to a tapestry of a full arm
sleeve, yet still somehow end up corporate,
behind the ink spilled, coffee stained,
highlighted and initialed contracts –
      I know for a fact I will not end up in HR
like my mother –
wearing black high heels and stockings, I go
back to school and get an internship this time,
Boston, give up and just become a lawyer
because I can analyze,

or Boston for babies and a Chestnut Hill house
with instead, a lawyer husband,
cooking chicken picada on Wednesdays and
pickle ball on Fridays after luncheons–
          I would stare at my wine glass and
remember the times I wrote –
before having the breakdown and booking my
one-trip ticket to Rome, because I once loved
it,EatPrayLove-ing my way down cobblestone
streets, closing my eyes when eating gelato,
nodding solemnly at the stuccos in the Uffizi or
sitting back down in San Clemente, asking the
heavens, they are tangible here, where my life
went.

I think, right now, I'm resigned to sticking to
what I know:
Nothing.

Well, nothing and poetry.

It Needs to Be Beautiful

Glass skin and the circles under your eyes are
gone,
A bag is heavy off one shoulder, the pack
swinging around to the front, grab the bottle
from the side-sleeve,
Put on the pot on the smoldering rocks, you
know how to cook a fire now,
There's a breeze coming off you like light,
jumping from stone to log,
An empty mind molded from total destruction –
this causes a smile,
Unfettered by yourself, relinquished from the
grime of your soul,
Scrape the soles of your shoes against the old
path,
Kicking off clogged dust is only an act, not a
metaphor,

My chest is heavy as I store this image in the tip
of my right pointer finger, I hope to touch the
lake with my nail and recollect this poem, far
away from itself right now.

Carly Simon's 'You're So Vain'

Fantastic song. Soundtrack to my life,
Because when you think that I'm alluding to
you,
I'm actually referencing my dead dog Spot,
And when I write about my cats,
I'm thinking of the love I lost in the third grade.

Everyone gets a cameo,
Therefore no one gets the spotlight,
And you can't point 'crazy' to your friends,
Unless you want to reveal some nasty truths,
That weren't even meant for you in the first
place.

So decode my meanings,
With your sleazy eyes,
And 'bruh girl' persona non-grata,
And mustached face, or too-hairy arms,
Red eyes and blue hair,
Wearing dirty jeans in the wintertime,
At your horse school, or with a bad tattoo,
Or doe eyes with viper fangs,
Hanging your sexuality from the rafters,
Judging with silence, black eye-liner and

An eyebrow piercing.
I see it all, boys and girls.

As Carly Simon said,
'you probably think this song is about you,
Don't you'.

Molting

The carcass of the bird, stiff, was placed in a
peculiar spot on my patio:
How did it get there?

Dead, it looked asleep, on its side, wings tucked
under the breast,
How a child sleeps positioned after a day at the
park.

Under the wooden bench built into the back
bones of the fence,
Some hands must have carried it, cupped, and
laid her gently down.

I found the thing the day I was going to meet
you.
The birds are watching my every move.

A month and a moon passed, I could not stand it,
I buried the bird under a bleached blossom,
withered from the heatwave.

Now, truth and freedom sting my tastebuds,
How weak was the witch who waded in these
boots, arches are not broken in.

She sent me the bluebird, I know it, on the day
of rebirth – a death.

Today, I found myself plucking off old feathers
from my goosebumped pores one by
One by one.
One more.

On the 101 Somewhere Right Before Salinas

where Steinbeck is from, and from this soil
tragic fictional flesh with names and greasy hair
grew up into pages and stories and best-sellers
all from the dry gold of the grass on the hills,
the ones I can never describe right,
the ones only Steinbeck got right
(and "got right" is the only way I can put it,
because to try and force poetry goes against the
feeling of that gold).

I was trying to space out and just drive
but love was walking in old stilettos all over my
heart
and I had a 48 hour migraine that was ebbing
and flowing
behind my right eye, which is now in the left as I
type,
and every man with testosterone that looked at
me in the right way
was haunting me on this drive, so I was singing
along to songs equal to this feeling,
when the silver Ram trunk put his hand out of
the window,
and started waving.

At first, rage perked up within my chest:
as another moment of my quiet femininity was
being interrupted,
looking in the rearview at the blonde in
sunglasses jamming down the road,
and his fingers started to dance one by one as if
to say "tootle-loo"
in the sleeziest way possible,
but,
the heat in my cheeks stalled,
and left out the crack in my sunroof,
and the shoes stopped tapping on my valves all
of a sudden:
I realized he wasn't looking in the rearview, or
being sleezy at all,
He was dancing his hand along the breeze of a
moving car,
Going 83 mph on a two-way road in Central
California.

Then all of a sudden I was Ramirez driving, read
R-4-MIREZ on the license plate,
and my fingers twitched because my car was a
silver Ram truck
and I was the car and was there in the backseat
as the dog
sniffing the air flowing in from the window

and I was the bug splattered on the windshield
and I was the glare of the sun
that hit me in my eye as I drove my car, behind
R4MIREZ, and gave me
the headache that was making me squint at the
individual blades of gold,
swaying, disappearing, collecting together
to make the mountains that we stared at,
as we all drove along the 101,
dancing along,
singing,
alone.

We are all alone together in the end.